# AUTISM
## MY LIFE ON THE SPECTRUM

**by Alex & Emily Christensen**
editing & design by Nathan Christensen

HWC PRESS

My name is Alex.

I have autism.

**When you have autism, people say you are "on the spectrum".**

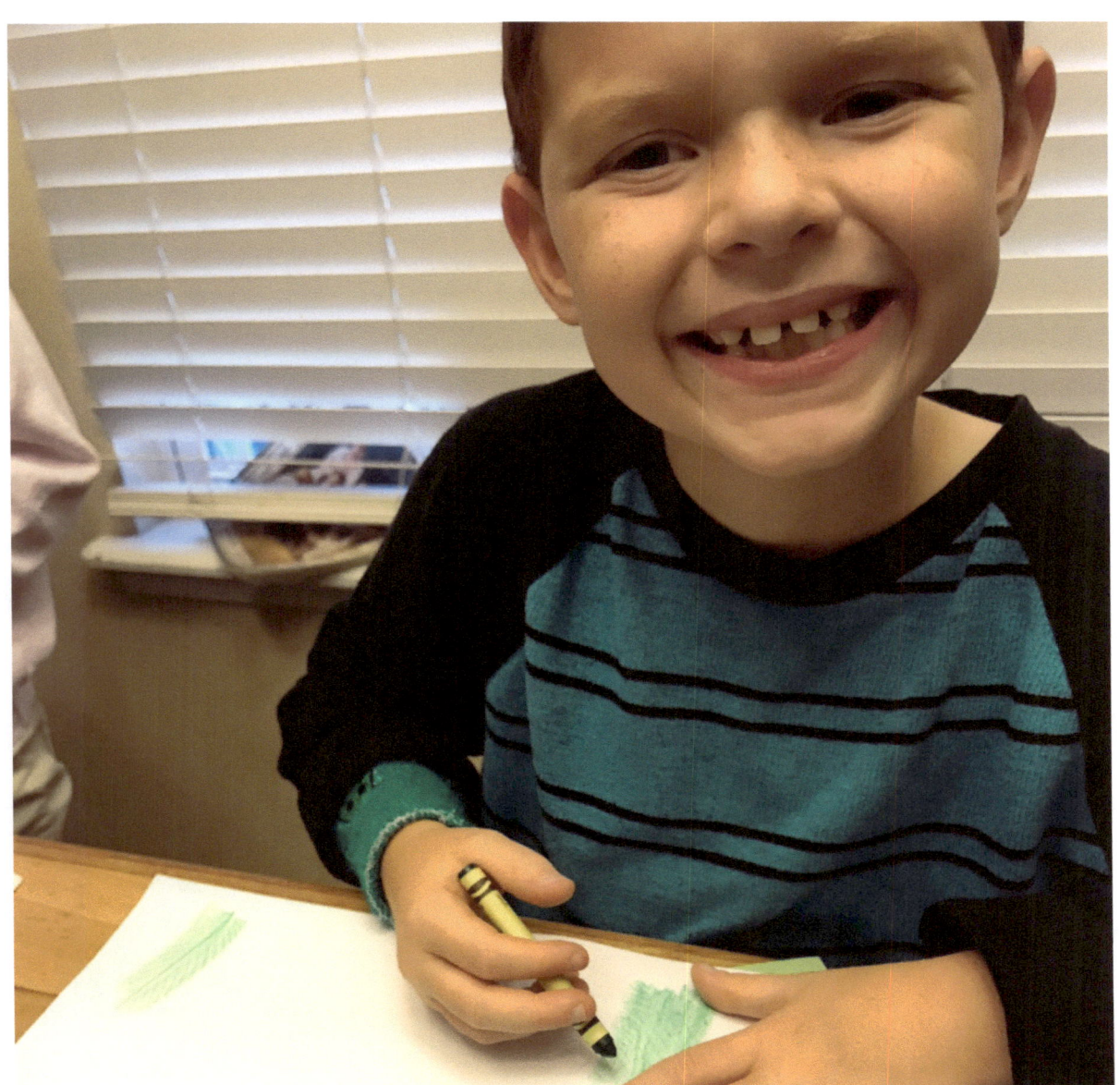

A spectrum is like a rainbow.

It has lots of colors.

**And autism is different for everybody.**

Some people on the spectrum need help getting dressed or brushing their teeth, or may have trouble speaking.

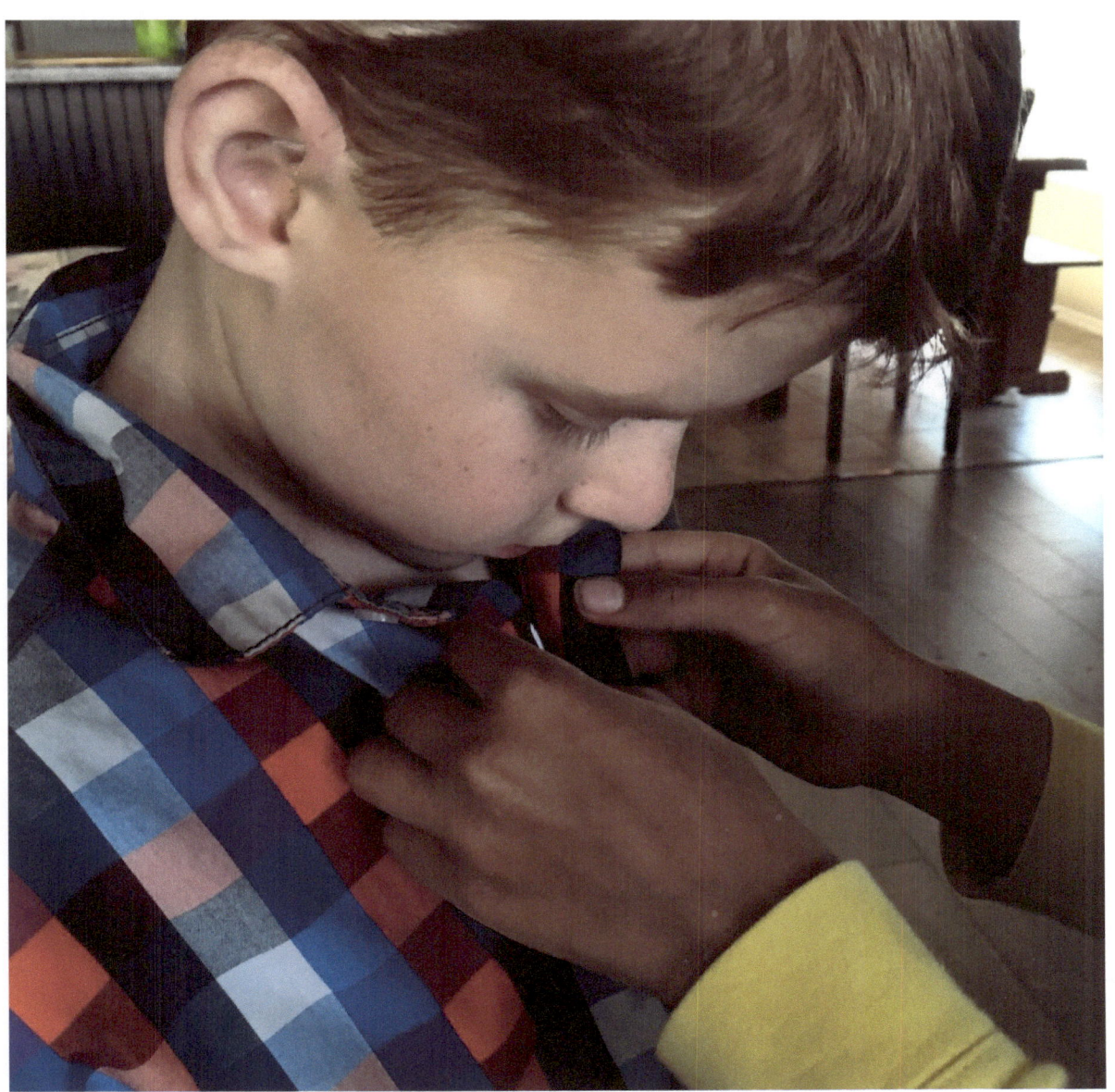

**Some people on the spectrum are scientists, or doctors, or artists, or billionaires.**

I'm somewhere in the middle.

**Where I am on the spectrum, I have to work on learning social skills that come easily to some people.**

Sometimes I say too much, and talk too loudly.

Sometimes I think something is funny, and no one else does.

**It can be hard for me to understand what people are saying with their faces.**

It can be hard for me to look people in the eyes.

Some people are confused by that.

**Where I am on the spectrum, there are some things I like to do over and over.**

Like flapping my hands.

Or making noises.

Or watching the same
part of a movie
again and again and again.

**Repeating things helps me to feel calm and safe.**

## Other things that make me feel safe are:

- Knowing what we will eat for breakfast tomorrow.

- Knowing which clothes I will wear next.

- Knowing what movie we will watch this weekend.

- Knowing how many days until my birthday.

## Things that do not make me feel safe are:

- Scratchy tags on itchy shirts.

- Bright lights and loud sounds.

- People who talk too fast.

- People who think I am being naughty, when really I just don't understand.

**Where I am on the spectrum, I can have trouble with language.**

When I was little, I would just echo back words, instead of making my own sentences.

Sometimes I talk for a long time, without giving the other person a chance to reply.

Sometimes my thoughts move so fast that I try to guess what somene wants, instead of listening to directions.

**But, you know what?**

**I also love
to make people laugh.**

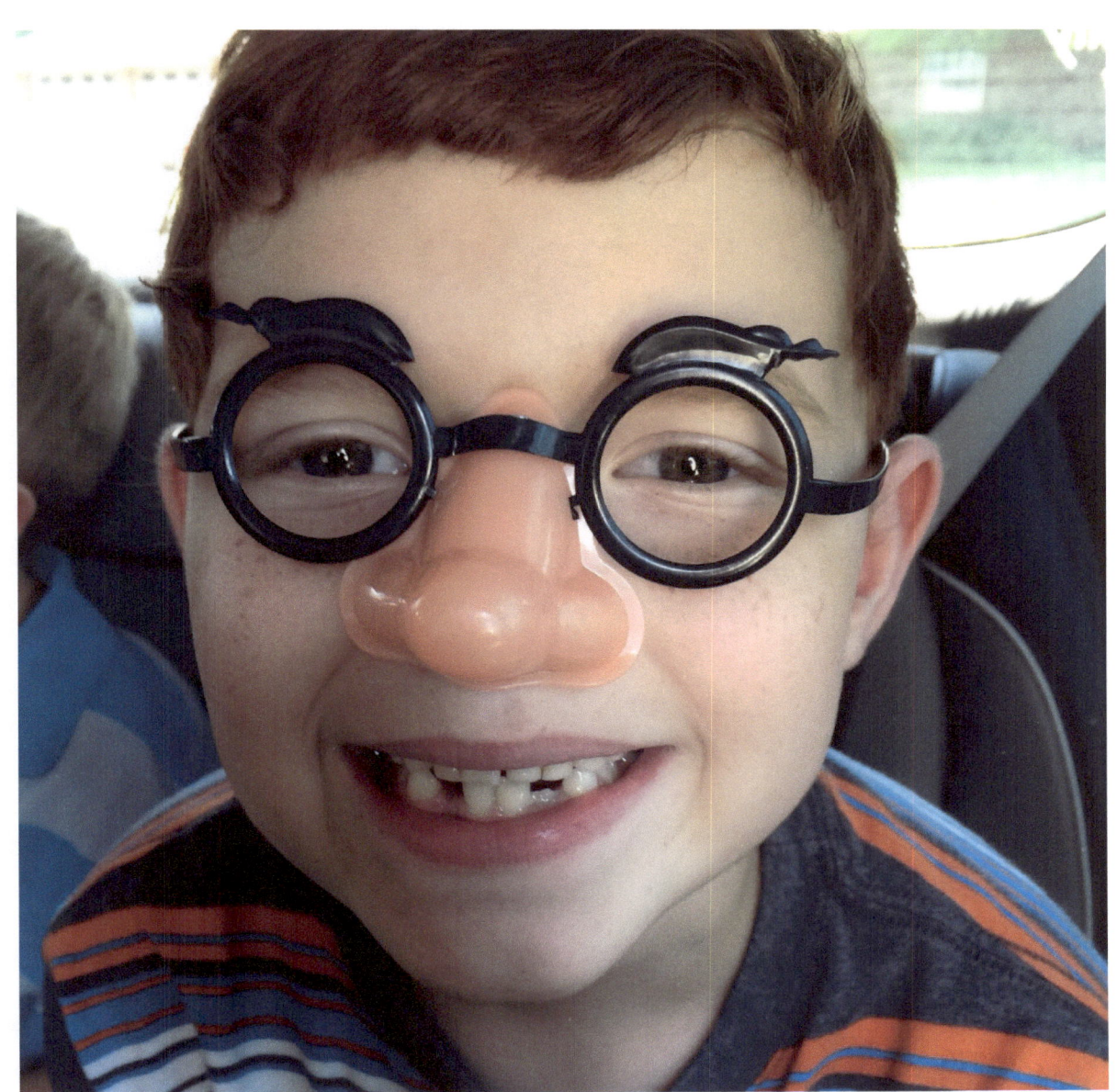

**And I have
a great imagination.**

And in my family,
I'm the best at
remembering song lyrics.

**Where I am on the spectrum, there are things that make me like everyone else, and things that make me different.**

**That's true for everyone on the autism spectrum.**

Just like it's true for everyone else!

I live my life
on the spectrum.

And it takes every color
of the spectrum
to make life beautiful.

Copyright © 2018 by Emily Christensen

Photography © 2018 by Emily Christensen

All rights reserved. This book or any portion thereof may not be reproduced or used in any manner whatsoever without the express written permission of the publisher except for the use of brief quotations in a book review or scholarly journal.

First Printing: 2018

ISBN: 978-1-948088-83-1

HWC Press, LLC
P.O. Box 3792
Bartlesville, OK 74006

housewifeclass@gmail.com
www.housewifeclass.com
@housewifeclass

Ordering Information:

U.S. trade bookstores and wholesalers, please contact HWC Press. Special discounts are available on quantity purchase by corporations, association, educators, and others.


About the typeface:

**Peace Sans**, designed by Sergey Ryadovoy
(www.behance.net/gallery/34760019/Peace-Sans-FREE-FONT)

www.ingramcontent.com/pod-product-compliance
Lightning Source LLC
Chambersburg PA
CBHW042030150426
43199CB00002B/18